The True Story of Cinderella
Really
and How She ^Became a Princess

By Deborah Hining, PhD

Illustrations by Nathan Johnson,
Michael Hining, & Mary Elizabeth

Published 2022, by Light Messages
www.lightmessages.com
Durham, NC 27713 USA
SAN: 920-9298

ISBN: 978-0-980-07569-4

Light Messages

To my mother and sister, both
Fairy Godmothers to many.

Thanks to all of you who have encouraged and indulged me in this little fantasy, especially to my family and my dear friends, Wally and Betty.

Once upon a time there was a girl named Cinderella who didn't like her life very much. She was an orphan, and so she felt lonely and unloved. Also, she had to have the world's worst job. It was hard, dirty work cleaning out fireplaces all day long, and as much as she tried to love her mean stepmother and her two demanding, ugly stepsisters, she found them all to be a constant trial. The worst of it was the painful boredom. Day after day of the same gray existence. She had nothing to do but work. Sometimes, when she grew desperate for something lively and bright she would catch mice and play with them. She even trained a pair of them to dance, and she spent hours laboring over tiny costumes for them.

She had dreams of becoming a Princess. She would sit in the ash heap in her free moments when no one was watching, usually when her two ugly stepsisters were taking their afternoon naps, and think about how lovely it would be to wear a clean dress every day and give tea parties for her loyal subjects. They would come to her with their problems, and she would dispense wisdom, and in return, hear how kind and good and intelligent she was.

When she arrived at the Fairy Godmother's domicile, she recognized it as the right place, for over the door, written in large, fancy letters were the words,

Prunella Gardenia Lucialla, FGM
Practicing Fairy Godmother

Board Certified in Fairy Godmother
and Associated Magic

Upon entering, she was surprised to find that the Fairy Godmother was a very ordinary looking middle-aged woman sitting in an office, surrounded by stacks of paper and adding machines. Her hair was done up in an untidy bun, and the only way Cinderella could tell that she might be a Fairy Godmother was the fact that a Magic Wand was stuck through the bun. Every time she nodded her head, fairy dust popped out of the end of the wand and swirled around her head. Other than that, she looked pretty much like an accountant. A Rolodex perched on one edge of the desk, and book of tax law sat on the other corner. The Fairy Godmother was muttering to herself and adding up a column of figures when Cinderella walked in.

"Hello, my dear," said the Fairy Godmother. "What can I do for you today?"

"I want to be a Princess," said Cinderella.

"Oh, a Princess? That's lovely. And why do you want to be a Princess?" The Fairy Godmother then proceeded to ask a number of surprisingly personal questions.

Cinderella told her about her family lineage, that her father had been an Earl and her mother a Duchess, and how her mother had died tragically when Cinderella was a little girl and how her father went broke trying to raise Cinderella in the manner in which she had been accustomed.

"But how could he possibly have spent all the money, my dear? Surely someone as wise and thoughtful as your father had life insurance on your mother to cover your needs in the event of such a disaster?"

"No," said Cinderella sadly. "My father didn't believe in life insurance then. He didn't realize how much my mother's staying home and keeping the house was worth."

"Oh, dear," said the Fairy Godmother. "And then what happened?"

"My father married my mean stepmother, and then a year later he died in a terrible car accident. So I was left with no one but this horrible woman and her two mean, ugly daughters. But I do my best," she said bravely. "No one can accuse me of not earning my keep."

"But why did you end up in the sole custody of your mean stepmother? Surely your father had a will which gave guardianship to someone who loved you. And didn't he leave you the manor house, or any assets on which you could live?"

"No," said poor Cinderella, as a tear slipped down her cheek. "He left everything to my stepmother because I was a minor, and he assumed she would take care of me. Besides, he had no idea he would die so young."

"What? No will? No guardianship? No trust or trustee or codicils or UTMAs? Who on earth was advising him?"

On the books illustration:

HOW TO BUILD YOUR OWN NEUCLEAR SUBMARINE

BY JOHNNY SMARTY PANTS —deceased.

SHARK TAMING MADE EASY

SKY DIVING for DUMMIES

"My stepmother," said Cinderella with a shrug. "She reads lots of books on How To Do Important Things All By Yourself, without using expensive professionals, and she's become quite an expert."

"Harrumph," said the FGM, and then, after a long pause in which she muttered to herself, she continued. "I do believe you could make quite a good Princess. You are kindhearted and hardworking, and you don't mind getting your hands dirty. You come from a background that will do. How about your education? Have you any training in Princessing?"

"Oh, yes!" Cinderella exclaimed, glad at last to have the right answer. I have read *How to Be a Princess in Ten Easy Lessons* a hundred times! I know it by heart!"

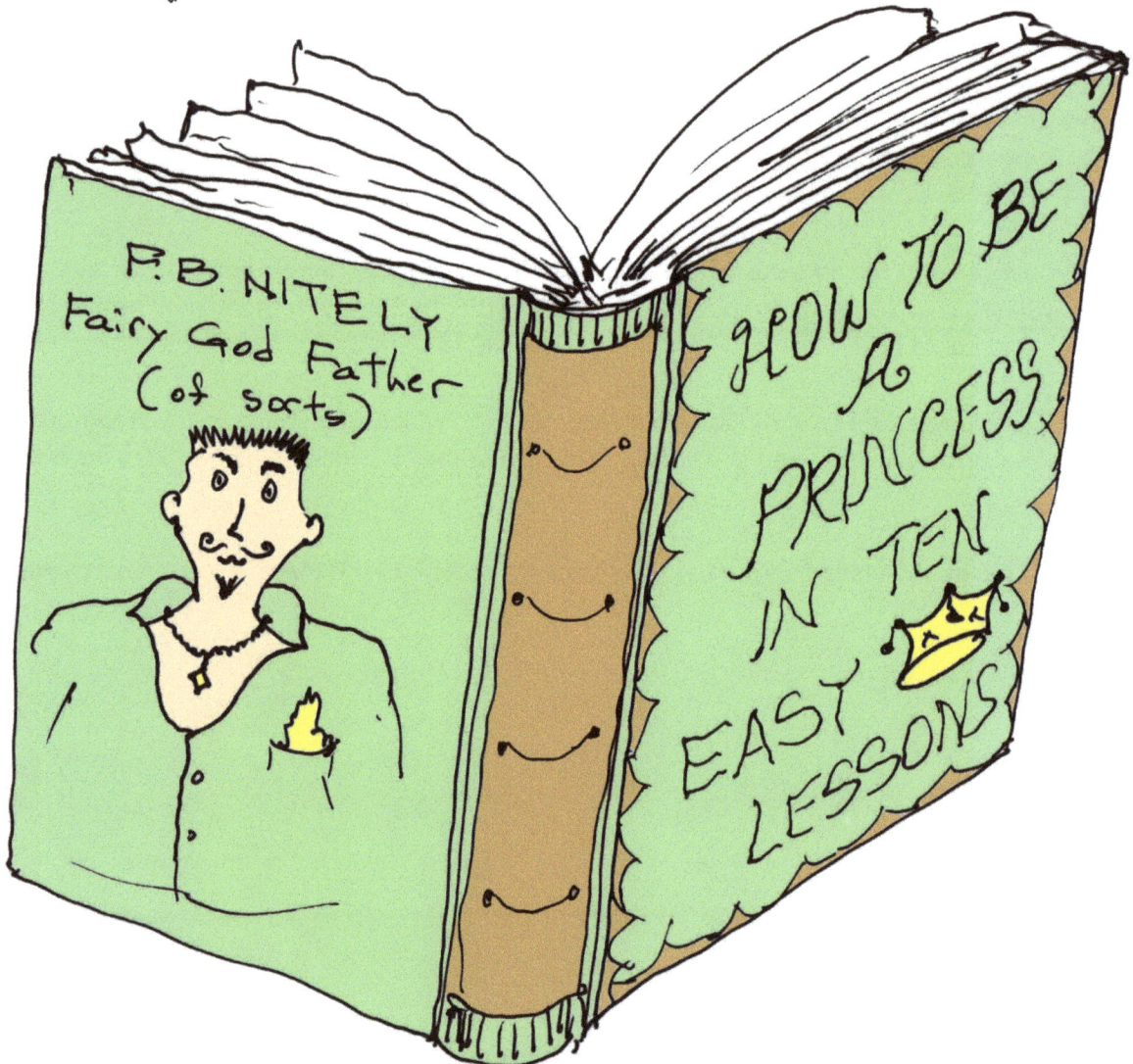

On the large book illustration:

P. B. NITELY
Fairy God Father
(of sorts)

HOW TO BE A PRINCESS IN TEN EASY LESSONS

"Hmm," replied the FGM thoughtfully, and she gave Cinderella a pat on the arm before she continued, "I know that book well, but I'm sorry to say that it was written by a charlatan, not a qualified Princess Trainer."

"But it was written by a Fairy Godfather," protested Cinderella. "He says so right in the introduction."

"Pfff!" exclaimed the the old woman, shaking her head. "Whoever heard of a Fairy Godfather? He's just making that up. Besides, he never earned his degree and he knew no magic at all. Go and look at the book again. You won't see the initials FGM, or even FGF after his name. He just pretended to know things. All this book teaches you is superficial things, like how to wave from a parade or how to keep hairspray from tarnishing your tiara, and a bunch of other stuff that is pure hogwash. To be a real Princess you have to know Important Things, like how to be diplomatic when you are facing the enemy of your people, or how to comfort a war-torn and impoverished country, or how to serve justice when justice seems futile. For that you have to have real schooling."

"Oh, dear," cried Cinderella. "That sounds hard!"

"Of course it's hard, darling. No one ever said Princessing was easy. That is, no one but the fellow who wrote that book. But don't worry, we'll manage somehow. I'm not a Fairy Godmother for nothing, and I love a challenge!

"I know you must have something in the way of assets, considering your background. And as hardworking as you are, you must have accumulated something during all this time you were working for your stepmother. What assets do we have to work with besides your good lineage, your excellent heart, and your strong work ethic?"

"Assets?" asked Cinderella, her heart sinking.

"Yes, you know, money you've saved up, maybe jewels your mother pinned to your diaper that you have forgotten about, a stock portfolio? That sort of thing."

"Do you have to have assets? Don't you just wave your wand?"

"My wand? Oh, my, yes!" exclaimed the Fairy Godmother. "But we have to have something to wave it over. You know, we can't create something out of nothing. And we can't go overdoing things now, can we, and wasting valuable resources. You want to save as much Magic as you can for future needs."

"Oh," said Cinderella, "I see," though she really didn't see at all. "Well," she continued slowly, thinking like mad. "I do have my pumpkin patch." She brightened. "And a pile of ashes in the back yard."

The Fairy Godmother stopped to think, "Hmm. Let me think. Where's my wand?" She looked around frantically, spilling fairy dust all over her desk.

"It's in your bun," pointed out Cinderella.

"Oh, yes. Thank you." She snatched it from her head and waved it around tentatively. "Now, let's see... you say you have a pumpkin patch... and... a pile of... ashes in the back yard. Hmmm." She waved her wand a little harder. "I don't see much hope for the ashes... Have you ever considered if you can get some sort of an income from those pumpkins?"

"Well, yes," said Cinderella. "I did try making pumpkin pies once, but nobody wanted them. I hate to admit it, but they weren't very good."

"Hmm," said the Fairy Godmother again. "Let's see those pumpkins." And off they went to Cinderella's pumpkin patch. They could hear Cinderella's ugly stepsisters snoring through the open window on the floor above. Her mean stepmother was down in the cellar counting her gold, as usual. They could hear the "clink, clink" as she piled coins on top of each other.

Cinderella's Fairy Godmother looked at the pumpkins, and said, "Oh, my dear! No wonder you had trouble selling those pies! These are not *pie* pumpkins. Pie pumpkins are small and round and have smooth flesh. These pumpkins are large and lovely and have stringy flesh. They are *carving* pumpkins, and some of the best I've ever seen! You've been using them for the wrong purpose! Let's take the best ones to market and see how much we get from them. That will give us a good start."

So Cinderella and her Fairy Godmother lugged the largest pumpkins to the market and put up a sign that said,

Beautiful, Large Pumpkins for Sale.!!! Make the Best Jack-O-Lanterns Ever!

And sure enough, the pumpkins sold in no time at all. It was helpful that it was just a couple of weeks before Halloween.

compost

"Now," said the Fairy Godmother, "This will get us started. You'll have to go to the market every day as they ripen, but be sure to save the seeds of the most beautiful ones. Don't use up all your resources in this one season. Getting you to Princesshood will take some doing. Now, go away and come back next week. By then I will have worked out a plan for you. Work that pumpkin patch, and make sure you water it well. And try working some ashes into the soil."

So Cinderella went away and picked pumpkins every day and sold them at the market. But she was careful to heed the advice of her Fairy Godmother, and she saved the seeds of the biggest, most beautiful ones, for she knew that she would need them for the next season. She was indeed a bright girl. The Fairy Godmother was right to see that she was Princess material.

The next week Cinderella went back to the FGM's office. When she arrived, the FGM was working on Cinderella's very plan. She could tell it was hers because it had sketches of thrones and scepters and crowns all over it. Cinderella felt her heart leap in her breast.

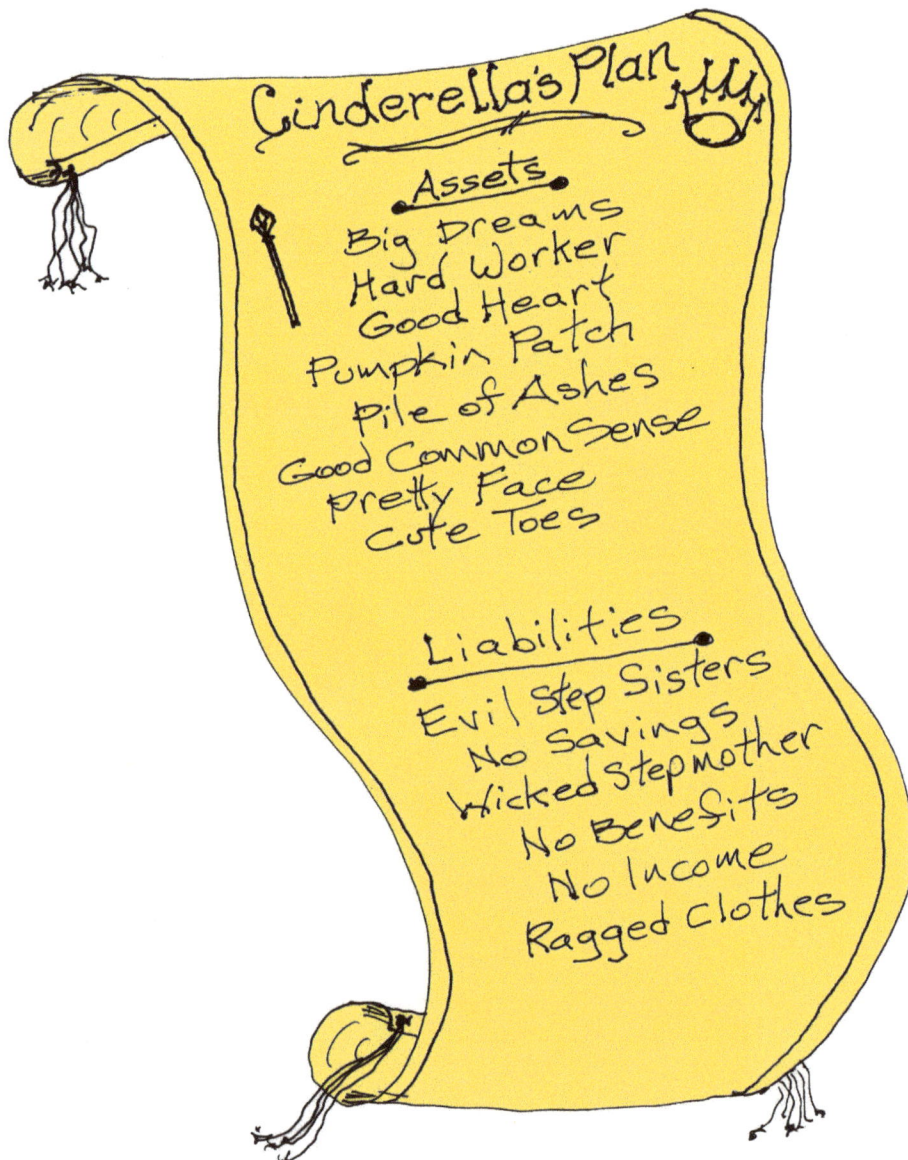

Cinderella's Plan

Assets
Big Dreams
Hard Worker
Good Heart
Pumpkin Patch
Pile of Ashes
Good Common Sense
Pretty Face
Cute Toes

Liabilities
Evil Step Sisters
No Savings
Wicked Stepmother
No Benefits
No Income
Ragged Clothes

"How's it going?" she asked hopefully.

"We've got a start," murmured the FGM thoughtfully. "Aside from the obvious question of getting you properly trained so you'll be prepared when you get the job, we have to think of how to get you there. Now which direction shall we take? I can think of three ways. Most Princesses are born to it—that's the easiest way, and by far the least risky, but frankly, I think we're a little late for that.

"You could marry a Prince, and that generally automatically makes you a Princess. Most people think that's the easiest way, but that's not my favorite. Sometimes these Princes turn out to be really bad husbands, and then you're stuck—or worse. Look what happened to poor Anne Bolyn, and that sweet Diana girl. Oh, dear, so many. If they had worked with me, I would certainly have discouraged taking that route. I can think of at least a hundred girls who came to bad ends because the Princes they believed in turned out to be perfectly rotten. This isn't a storybook, you know. This real life, and you have to be careful. You don't marry just to become a Princess. Your heart has to live in your husband's breast, and his has to live in yours before you can find happiness as a Princess in that way."

"I wouldn't mind marrying a Prince," murmured Cinderella, blushing, "If he really were a True Prince." In fact, Cinderella had actually dreamed of that very thing many, many times, mainly because she was constantly aware of being lonely and unloved, and having a Prince as a husband somehow seemed right to her. But she never really thought it could be a possibility.

"I know, dear," replied the Fairy Godmother kindly. "And a Prince may be in your future yet. But we don't want your success dependent on the whims of a man. No, I think the best way is for you to do it the straightforward way, and just go for the job. It's a sad fact that a band of Dragons came through here a few years back and ate up most of the Princesses, so there is a shortage. You can benefit from that, you know, as sad as it is.

"It's risky, of course, in terms of your assets, and there's a good chance you could lose principal before all is said and done. But at least you won't get your heart broken. There are a couple of ways to go about it. You could either be elected by general election, or you can go directly to the King and Queen and apply for the job. Different Kingdoms have different methods. You have a real good chance either way, what with your pretty face and your kind heart. That always is good for votes in an election. But you'd need to mount quite a campaign to get your name out there, and right now, you really don't have enough money to do it successfully. We could try that later if we have to. But I'm thinking that we can... just maybe, if the market for pumpkins holds a few days longer, and if we can find some things on sale, and wait a minute, let me add up these numbers again." And she thought and thought, and added up some numbers on her adding machine, and waved her Magic Wand really hard over the papers.

11

At last she said, "Well, considering all our options and the resources we have, I think we should go for the first available opening since they don't come along that often. Mind you, we're a little short, and the risk is more than I would like for you to take, but we can hedge a little, and in a year or two you could run for office if it doesn't work out. Are you willing to take that kind of risk?"

"Really?" asked Cinderella. "Is that possible?"

"Of course," said the Fairy Godmother. "You're a lovely girl, bright enough to learn Princessing skills. You work hard, you have a good, kind heart, a good enough lineage, and underneath all that dirt is a very pretty face. Now I happen to know there is a King and Queen in the next village who is giving a ball next month for the express purpose of finding themselves a Princess. I think they were sort of hoping they could get their son, the Prince, to find himself a bride so they could take care of two problems at once—you know, having both a daughter-in-law to give them grandchildren and getting a Princess to take off some of the workload of the Queen, who's thinking of cutting back. Poor things lost their own Princess to particularly nasty Dragon about 5 years ago. But the girl—bless her—was a fighter, and managed to stick her embroidery needle in the roof of the Dragon's mouth as she went down. He couldn't eat again after that. He starved to death after a few weeks.

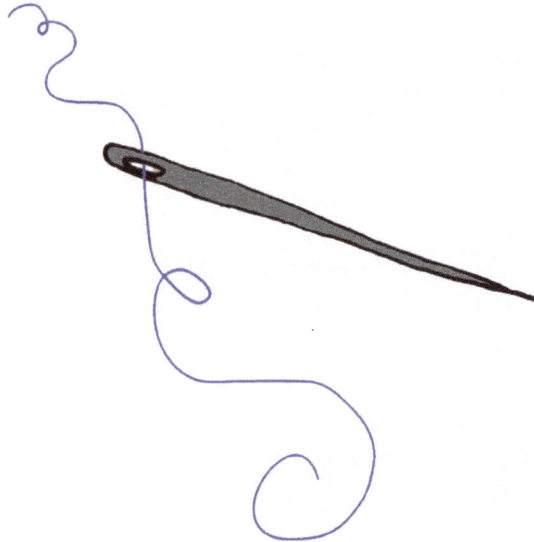

"But their son is very picky, and has been taking his own sweet time. So they've decided to go ahead and look for a Princess on their own and not wait for him. Now, if that's agreeable to you, we'll get started right away. Are you ready to begin? It's going to take some doing to impress this particular Queen after having had the daughter she did."

Cinderella's head was spinning. She hadn't counted on Dragons and stepping into the place of such a courageous Princess. "Well," she said slowly, scratching at the lice in her armpit. "Do you think it will be easy to get the King and Queen to like me?"

The Fairy Godmother looked at her carefully, then sighed and said slowly, "Well, we have a lot of work to do." She went back to her adding machine, muttering to herself. Waving her Magic Wand over the figures a few times, she added them up again and shook her head.

"It's going to be a challenge coming up with enough assets to make this happen," she sighed. "There's the training, and then we need to get you a designer dress and get your hair and nails done, and we have to have shoes. Good ones that are comfortable enough for you to dance far into the night. And they have to look really good. The Queen notices these things, and although the King doesn't give a fig about shoes, the Queen may just turn her thumbs down if your feet don't look good. She has a thing about feet."

"Oh," said Cinderella, "how do you know these things?"

"It's my job to know," said the FGM. "I learned in it basic Queen Deciphering my first year at FGM school."

"Is that Magic?" asked Cinderella breathlessly.

"Not hardly," said the Fairy Godmother. "I mean it's not common knowledge, but the real Magic comes in when it gets more complicated. You should see me when I start working with tax credits. I even impress myself sometimes. But that's way beyond what you need now. What we need now is more assets to work with. Come on, surely you have a diamond pendant your mother tucked in one of your booties? Or your father maybe left a few personal items in a handwritten will he forgot to mention?"

Cinderella hung her head. "No, nothing. Nothing at all. Except, except, well..."

"What is it?"

"Well, I have these trained mice...."

"Trained mice? What have you trained them to do? "

"I dress them up in fancy ball clothes and they dance the minute waltz up on their little hind legs like people."

"They dance the minute waltz on their hind legs? Do they hold each other in their arms and twirl around and keep time with the music?"

"Of course. They are very smart mice."

"That's wonderful! Are you willing to rent them out? Can you train more?"

"Well, I suppose..."

"Wonderful! Go get them as quickly as you can. I have to catch a flight to Paris!"

"So Cinderella ran home and fetched her mice. When she returned, she saw that the FGM had her bag packed. The FGM took one look at the pitiful cage the mice were in, and in a desperate sweep of her hand, waved her wand over it. The smashed and crooked wire was transformed into a lovely gilded cage, complete with trills and flourishes and little prisms that caught the light and twinkled on the mice's costumes

"I'll be back, my dear! Come see me tomorrow!" And off she went in a puff of fairy dust.

The next day Cinderella met her just as she was returning from her journey. She looked very wrinkled and frumpy, but she had a smile on her face.

"What happened?" asked Cinderella.

"Oh, I hate this jet lag. I always get it going from East to West. I was hoping the trip would be so short I wouldn't have time to get it, but this time it seems worse than ever. This is the last time I ever go to Paris. They make those seats smaller every time I fly, and oh, my feet have swollen. I'm just going to have to go back to school and learn Magic Carpeting. This will be the death of me."

"WHAT HAPPENED?" shouted Cinderella. She could hardly stand her excitement.

"Oh, my dear, I have leased your mice out to the Paris Rodent Circus for the next year. They loved them! And they said they could take two more pair, if you can teach them the tango. And they have paid you enough money to send you to Princessing School! You can get a degree in Princessing!"

"A degree in Princessing? What about the ball?"

"Oh, yes, of course, first things first. We may still be a little short, if we set aside the whole four years' tuition, but we really should, because if you have to be elected, you'd better be darned sure you are qualified before running. The King and Queen may give you the job just because you touch their hearts in just the right way. But the general public is going to be more demanding."

"And I wish we had more time. We could put this money in a good growth fund and you might have enough in a few years to get the perfect dress and the shoes and the haircut and oh my goodness, you'll need a nice car to get to the ball, but most of this money will be needed for the education. Oh, I don't like dealing in short-term investment cycles. We'll just have to forego the Diamond Tiara."

"Diamond Tiara?" asked Cinderella, growing excited. "Can I have a Diamond Tiara? A Princess surely needs a Diamond Tiara!"

"No dear, you can't afford a Diamond Tiara. It's too big an extravagance, and we can't waste resources. You can save up the money and buy yourself a Diamond Tiara after you become a Princess. That job pays really well, you know."

But Cinderella was now wanting a Diamond Tiara really, really badly. She had read about how beautiful they are in the book on *How To Be a Princess in Ten Easy Lessons*, and she had seen several styles featured that she would love to own. Besides, she knew how to keep hairspray from ruining them really well by now. Before she knew it, she was envisioning herself in a parade wearing the three pronged style with the little dangly things. Unconsciously, she lifted her hand in a Grand Princess Wave.

"Oh, please, can I please, please have a Diamond Tiara? I've always wanted one! And it will make me feel like a real Princess."

"Absolutely not. If you get the Diamond Tiara, you can't afford a Vera Wang dress. And the Queen will certainly notice if you don't wear a designer dress. She will scratch your application as sure as I'm standing here if you show up in something off the rack."

"I hear there are such things as credit cards," said Cinderella. "Couldn't I buy a Diamond Tiara with a credit card and then pay it back after I become a Princess?"

Now the Fairy Godmother's face darkened. "Credit Card?" said the FGM with a certain tone in her voice that Cinderella found a little chilling. "CREDIT CARD? EXCUSE ME? 'Credit card' is a bad word around here. You are never, ever allowed to use a credit card to buy such things as Diamond Tiaras. Don't you know what the interest rate is on those things? Princesses have enough sense not to get in credit card debt. If you expect me to work with you, you must promise me never to even think of racking up credit card debt. If you can't pay them off each month, you can't have one. Period." And she crossed her arms in a huff and glared at Cinderella. Her head trembled so that fairy dust showered all around like a little rainbow halo.

Poor Cinderella. She had never seen anyone so upset since the time Drudgella and Dumbella both got a crush on the same boy and duked it out over who got to dance with him first. Neither one got to dance with him because he fled when he discovered the fight was over him, and he had not been seen in these parts since. Both the sisters still blamed each other.

"I'm sorry," said Cinderella hanging her head. "I'll forget about credit cards."

"All right, then," said the FGM, softening. "Now we have to get to work. First, Princessing training. And we have only three weeks, so we'll have to get a tutor for a crash course in the basics. You really must get your four-year degree, but you can start that after the ball. If you can convince the King and Queen—but particularly the Queen—that you are good Princess material, they may want you to serve an apprenticeship before hiring you officially. You'll need to use that time to at least get through your first year, and hope that nobody makes real demands on you for another couple of years."

"A crash course?" asked Cinderella with a gulp. Between working the pumpkin patch and keeping Drudgella and Dumbella polished up, she wasn't getting enough sleep already. When would she find the time to study? She expressed her concern to the FGM.

"Hmm, I see what you mean," mused the FGM. "Well, if you're really committed, maybe you should take the plunge and quit your ash-hauling job. The pay is lousy anyway, and there are no benefits, so you'd might as well be self-employed. You'd do better with the pumpkins and the mice. You could even branch out and try pie pumpkins, since Thanksgiving is coming up."

"That's a great idea!" shouted Cinderella. "You're brilliant, Fairy Godmother!"

"Oh, just a little minor Magic," replied the FGM, blushing. "Anyway, we've wasted enough time, so we'd better get going. I've been thinking about this, and I believe that the best person to tutor you would be Professor Von Heinstein. He's retired from the College of Royal Empiricism, used to be the head of Princess Studies. Now he consults when practicing Princesses have been promoted to Queening, if it's been a long while since they took their last course. He's been more immersed in Queening lately, but he still is one of the best in Princessing. Come on, we'll get you signed up."

"Can I afford this?" asked Cinderella.

"You can't afford not to. He's not cheap, but you want to be the best, don't you? And the only way to be the best is to learn from the best. Now come on!"

So Cinderella became the protégé of the famous Professor Von Heinstein. She turned in her notice to the mean stepmother, who was quite perturbed over the fact that she gave only one week's notice. Cinderella was inclined to just walk out, but the Professor insisted that Princess Integrity be maintained. One week was the bare minimum to resign from hauling ash.

During the mornings, she tended to her pumpkin patch and took care of the mice. The tango was proving to be a bit tricky, but she could see progress.

In the afternoons she learned Intelligent Conversationing, Diplomacy with Curmudgeons, International Affairs, and Princess Hygiene, Carriage and Diction. She could see progress in herself, too. Within a week, she had learned to walk right and talk right and carry on an Intelligent Conversation about International Affairs with the most crotchety of Curmudgeons, and to bathe every single day. The professor let her skip Embroidery and Unicorn Taming since they probably wouldn't be needed for some time yet. After two weeks, Cinderella was definitely shaping up nicely.

Three days before the ball, the Fairy Godmother told her it was time to begin the final preparations.

"I see you are looking much more Princessy, my dear," she told her, "And now we can put on the final touches. I have set an appointment with Bruce, who will do your hair and makeup for the ball."

"Is Bruce a Fairy Godmother?"

"No, he's a Hair Fairy, more of a specialist, while Godmothers are generalists. He minored in makeup, too, so I would consider him enough of an expert to take care of that as well. You're pretty enough so that you don't need much Magic there. The hair needs to be really special, though, and he's unparalleled in that department. The Queen has a thing for hair. Hair and shoes. She'll no doubt look you over from head to toe. Especially head *and* toe."

Bruce turned out to be a lovely gentleman, younger than Cinderella had expected, and he definitely was an Expert Hair Fairy. After his initial consternation, where he nearly wept at the sight of Cinderella's split ends, he picked up his Magic Wand, which looked exactly like a brush, except for the fairy dust that puffed out of the end each time he flicked his wrist, which was often, and went to work.

He washed and cut and dried and curled her hair, then put it up in the most charming Princessy Do that Cinderella could imagine. Then he did her nails and her face, and when he was done, Cinderella looked into the mirror and was shocked and amazed at what she saw there. Even the Princesses pictured in the *How to Be a Princess in Ten Easy Lessons* did not begin to compare with the face that gazed back at Cinderella from Bruce's mirror. He had truly worked Magic!

Bruce was satisfied. The Fairy Godmother was satisfied. Professor Von Heinstein stroked his beard in satisfaction. But no one was as satisfied as Cinderella. She glowed with pleasure.

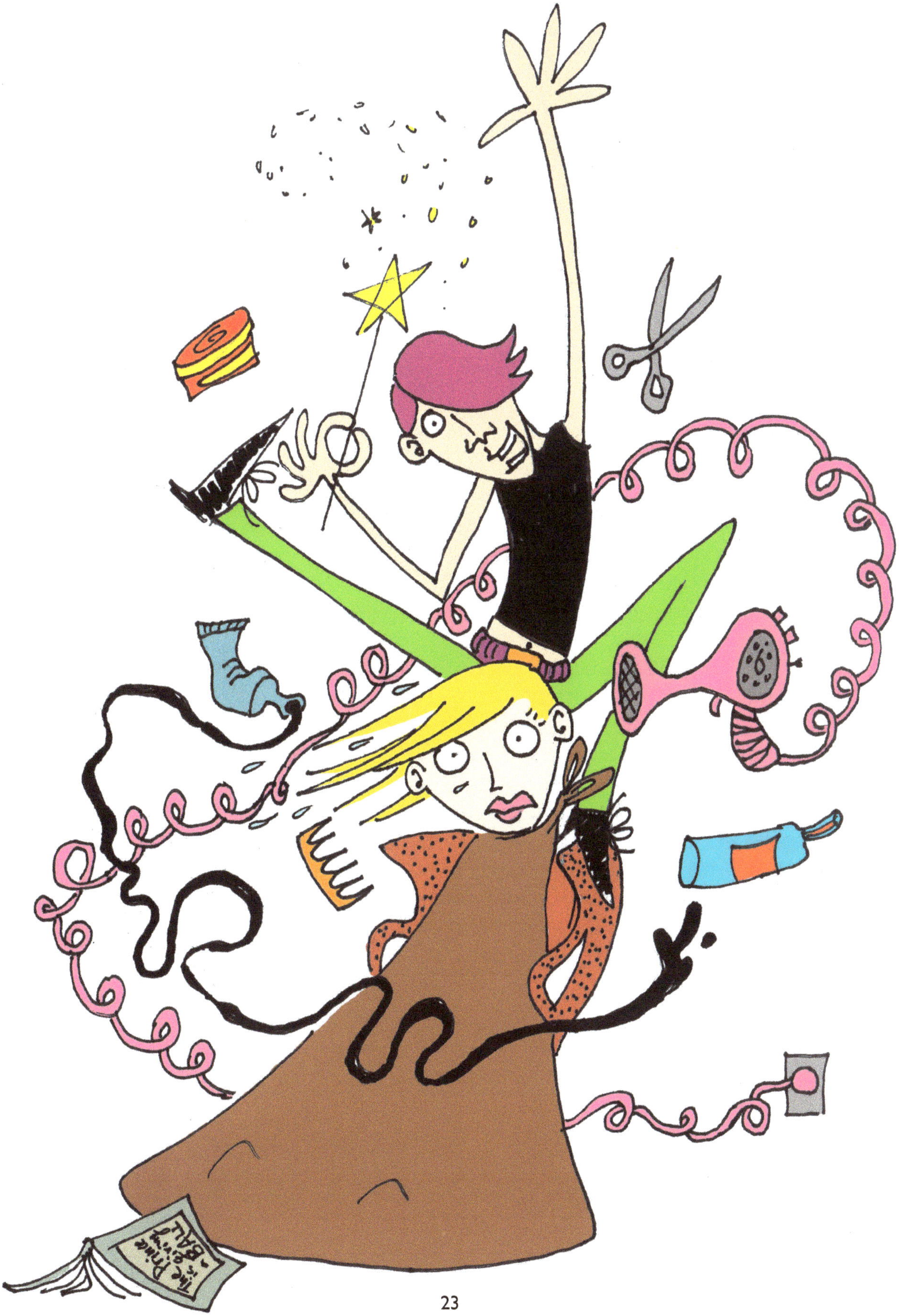
The Prince
is giving
a BALL

"Now," said the Fairy Godmother. "I don't know how you will feel about this, but I want to show you something," and she marched Cinderella down to the local Goodwill and asked the lady at the counter to show her the dress she had put on hold there.

"I happened to find this yesterday, and it is a Valentino original. I can't imagine how it ended up here, but if you like it, it will save you enough so that you can maybe rent a Diamond Tiara for tomorrow evening. What do you think?"

And out came the most beautiful blue Princessy Dress that Cinderella had ever seen or imagined.

It was all spangly and sparkly and frothy, and all in the best of taste. Cinderella clapped her hands with glee. In that dress she could surely be the most Princessy of all the Princesses in the world!

"It's last year's, but, see, it's never been worn—the tags are still on it—no doubt donated by the store or something. I don't think the Queen will notice, though. She will be concentrating on the, you know, head and toe. And the King's favorite color is blue. Do you like it?"

"Like it??" exclaimed Cinderella. "It's the most magnificent Princess Dress I have ever, ever seen, even in the books! I'll take it!"

And so she bought the dress, and after that, they went to the shoe store and bought the soon-to-be-famous Glass Slippers which were also comfortable enough to dance far into the night in. Since she had enough money left to rent a Diamond Tiara for the evening, she was able to have her cake and eat it too, so to speak. I mean, she didn't actually eat anything, that's just an expression, which means she got to do exactly what she wanted. She got the dress, the shoes, and the tiara.

"Now, just one more thing, dearie," said the FGM. "You need a car to get to the ball. You have enough money to buy an 8 year old Ford Fairlane, which would be great, because you'll have to have transportation on your election campaign if tomorrow evening doesn't pan out, or you can rent a Rolls Royce for just the evening. What do you think?"

"What would the Queen like the best?"

"I see your point, although I think the King will be the one who is more interested in the car you arrive in. He's something of an aficionado. We'll worry about campaign transportation later if it comes to that."

The next few hours both flew and dragged, if you can imagine such a dichotomy. But after much anguish and feeling like the time would never arrive, suddenly it was time to go to the ball, and Cinderella wished she had a few more hours to get ready. But already the Rolls was parked at her door, chauffeured by a mousy looking little man, and Bruce was fussing over the last bit of stray hair and tucking it into her gorgeous Diamond Tiara with the three prongs and the little dangly things, and she looked into the mirror and wished, oh, she wished all kinds of things that I won't go into here. You can just imagine what she was wishing as she looked into the mirror and prepared herself for the ball as fairy dust swirled around her head and made her feel all dreamy.

"Now, remember, dear, the Rolls and tiara are rented only until 12:30, and anyway, no decent Princess would dream of staying out later than that on the first ball—you know you have to have some intrigue. So be sure you are out of there before the clock strikes midnight, or we will lose your deposit."

"Yes, Fairy Godmother," said Cinderella dreamily, though she hardly heard her, even as she gave her last minute advice on what to say during the interview. She was too busy wishing.

So Cinderella went to the ball, and of course you've heard the story of how the Prince, who had pretty much given up on finding a bride because he hadn't found a girl who was both kind and beautiful enough, laid eyes on Cinderella and immediately fell in love. In fact, he ignored all the other girls and kept dancing with Cinderella over and over again, which technically is very rude and not becoming to a Prince at all, but the fact is he was so smitten that we have to forgive him.

And the King and Queen were also quite impressed because Cinderella danced the minute waltz so perfectly in her dainty Glass Slippers, and she was dazzling in her blue, shimmery dress and her Diamond Tiara, and she was able to converse so Intelligently on Matters of Import, and she smelled so good.

Actually, everyone was mightily impressed. So the King and Queen decided to hire her on the very spot, even before Cinderella had a chance to hand in her application, and before they realized that the Prince thought she was really hot, as they say these days. So it turned out to be just lovely every way around.

Then there was all that mushy stuff about the Prince and Cinderella dancing in the moonlight and gazing into each others' eyes with longing, but if I go into all that, you might say, "yuk," so I'll just skip that part.

Before Cinderella knew it, the clock was striking midnight, and she all of a sudden remembered that she was supposed to be gone by then. The fact that the FGM was standing at the door and waving madly at her jogged her memory. Suddenly she felt the panic rise, and she made a mad dash out the door and to the waiting Rolls with the mousy little chauffeur waiting with the door open.

Unfortunately, she tripped and fell on her way down the stairs, losing the soon-to-be-famous Glass Slipper and ripping her dress. She also fell splat into a mud puddle, and I can tell you, she looked more like the Cinderella of old more than she looked like a Princess at that moment. But she gathered herself up and leapt into the car and they sped off into the night just as the Prince was barreling down the steps to the palace, shouting,

"Wait! I don't even know your name!"

Anyway, the rest is history, which you should know, if you have read your history books as you should have. To remind you of the facts, the King, Queen, and Prince tracked Cinderella down through a trusty footman, who discovered the right foot for the abandoned shoe, and Cinderella came to live in a beautiful little house near the castle so the King and Queen could get to know her better, and she and the Prince became engaged. But Cinderella, heeding the advice of her FGM, insisted on delaying the wedding until she was assured of earning her Princesshood on her very own and until the Prince proved to her that he was, indeed a True Prince with an Honest and True Heart. She finished her four years of Princess School in just two and a half years on the accelerated plan. She had to take heavy loads, and she had to go to summer school, but she was used to hard work, and after all, was a very bright girl to boot.

So Cinderella married the Prince, moved into the Palace and was dutifully sworn in before taking up the role of Lifetime Princess. She never gave up her Pumpkin and Mouse enterprise, on the advice of the FGM, just so she would have something to fall back on. She and the Prince lived happily and prosperously ever after as regular clients of the FGM and referred their friends and families to her.

With her help, the King and Queen were able to fulfill their lives' secret dream of transforming one corner of the Palace grounds into a Magic Kingdom (much better than the one down in Florida, by the way, because it really was Magic) for children with sad illnesses who needed to spend a day or two being happy. They built it in honor of their own lost daughter and had a special, thrilling ride named "The Needle," which reminded everyone of her courage, and the whole venture made them glad because they knew they were making a difference in the world. The Prince's footman became her client, too. His dream was to open his own chain of shoe stores, and the FGM was able to help him buy a franchise and then improve on it.

As for the mean stepmother, she didn't want to see the FGM because she thought she charged too much, and she figured she could do it all on her own. She then made the unfortunate mistake of buying a book about how to get rich quick, written by the same fellow who wrote the book about Princessing that Cinderella had so carefully read. She followed tip number 8: "Investing as a Venture Capitalist in a Start-up Tech Company." Needless to say, she was broke within the year.

The two stepsisters wanted to engage the FGM, but she refused to take them as clients. They both wanted to be Miss America, but the FGM said their hearts were in the wrong place. All they wanted was to be beautiful and wave in the parades. They never said anything about World Peace. Besides, even they didn't have enough resources, and the FGM didn't have enough Magic, to make them beautiful, even with the expert help of Dr. Beautimous, the world famous plastic surgeon.

So in the end, everybody got what they deserved, and that is the end of this, the True Story of Cinderella and How She Really Became a Princess.

THE END

About the Author

The author, Deborah Griffitts Hining, is grateful that she has spent her whole life in magical places, surrounded by Fairy Godmothers and knights in shining armor. She hopes that she has learned a thing or two from them about enabling others to make their dreams come true. Like Cinderella, she was taught by willing nurturers to leverage her assets and mix in good old-fashioned hard work to achieve her goals. A Tennessee native, she received her undergraduate and Master's degrees from the University of Tennessee at Knoxville, and completed her PhD in Renaissance Dramatic Literature from Louisiana State University.

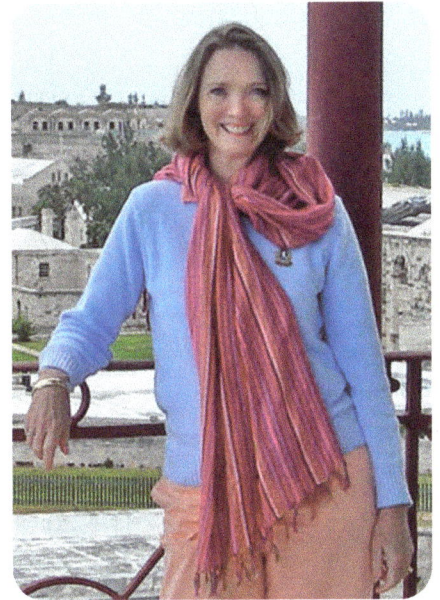

Deborah's flare for the creative has followed her throughout her life. In 1980, she and three of her best friends co-founded Playmakers of Baton Rouge, a professional repertory company for young audiences. From the beginning, she served as actor, director, writer, and Jill-of-all-trades. In 1981 she won the David Library American Freedom Award as co-author of a play, *All the Music We Played Here*, but that distinction paled in comparison to the birth of her first baby in the same year. During the next few years, she continued to write and she taught speech performance courses at the University of North Carolina in Greensboro and Chapel Hill while spending most of her creative energy on her vocation as Mom to her daughter, Mary Elizabeth, and son, George.

In 1993, Deborah decided to use her creative energy and skills to help others realize their dreams. She became a financial planner and quickly attained the designations of CFPR, ChFC, CLU, and CRPC. She has spent the last 7 years concentrating on developing processes to help people understand what they really want from life so that she can help them honor their dreams and become motivated enough to achieve them.

Today, Deborah continues that mission by helping others reach their full potential by encouraging them to believe in themselves and what they are capable of attaining. *The True Story of Cinderella and How She Really Became a Princess,* is one of the many fruits of Deborah's dream to serve as a Fairy Godmother to those she encounters along life's journey.

Other works by Deborah include *Money is No Object. It's Not the Subject Either*.

The author lives in North Carolina, with her husband Michael and enjoys traveling, gardening, and rescuing derelict old houses. She can be reached at dhining@gmail.com.